You Be the Music.. I'll Be the Lyrics

Rena Wilson

pencil

ISBN 978-93-5458-912-6

Published in India 2021 by Pencil

A brand of
One Point Six Technologies Pvt. Ltd.
123, Building J2, Shram Seva Premises,
Wadala Truck Terminal, Wadala (E)
Mumbai 400037, Maharashtra, INDIA
E connect@thepencilapp.com
W www.thepencilapp.com

Author biography

Being a hopeless romantic, in a world filled with people scared to love, is heartbreaking at best. Music and poetry fill my hopeless soul, in desire that one day, someone will find my soul beautiful and timeless...until then, my twin flame will always remain my most passionate dream.

For you---you may never know who you are....

CONTENTS

Foreword

Thank you for reading parts of my soul. May you always find the lyrics in everything that you do.

Acknowledgements

First of all, I would like to thank all of the many people in my life that have been there for me. If you asked me to read something, or just simply listened to my reading. I appreciate you. To that someone special that pushed me to keep writing and publish this book, you mean the world to me. Without you telling me how much my poetry meant, I would have never known. You have been the inspiration behind my motivation. Much mad love to you.

Introduction

In pursuit of a love like the movies, I dream in vivid color. The love that we need isn't always the love that we receive. In no truer words, Kevin Gates says, "Go where you are celebrated, not tolerated." I hope that you find the love and passion behind my words. Take what means something to you, and leave the rest. Love and light always. Enjoy the words and lyrics, let them light up your soul. This poetry is about different adventures I have had over a lifetime. It's about feeling something so strongly that it eats you alive when the lights go down at night. It's also about love, sex, and music. Let's get lost.

Flames burn out- or get gas thrown on them

Link

I see you for who you are

Guess that means I'm about done

Each time you take from me

The less my heart even needs

You're selfish with your own nature

Leaving my emotions to bleed

It won't be too much longer

And the rest is history

Because I don't hold on to that

And that is my story.

I waited for you to chase me

To even give me half of you

Ive looked for the day

When I was what you'd choose

I don't really have much left

Tired of trying to make it work

Because in the end

I always loved like I'd never been hurt.

Can we just pretend we're still friends

And make the most of this night

Meet up in a room somewhere private

There's no need to fight it

You can undress me

Piece by piece.

As I breathe in and breathe out

While you use your teeth

I'll caress your skin

My smooth hands charting a path

We can worry about it tomorrow

When we face the aftermath

My hands have longed for you

I'm burning with desire

For a second pretend you love me

Help to extinguish my fire

Your skin could be this paper

Your lips could be this ink

I could finally write a masterpiece

Just from this one link.

The pain you give me

I hate to think you're playing me

But I dont think you know

From the minute I see you

To the feelings I don't show

The way I hold my breath

Until I see you again

Makes me think it's a phase

A game I'll never win

I tell myself I'm feeling too much

I don't want to push you away

But I think we could make this something

If you really wanted to stay

You don't know how loyal I am

Or the way you take my breath

How I would be your everything

Give my all til there's nothing left

Because I daydream of you

And wonder how you are

How sitting beside me in a room

Is still just too far

How I want to hold your hand

And never let you go

How I wish you'd just be real with me

And want to let me know

It's that I feel so infatuated

Everytime we meet up

How it's strange that I fight this feeling

When I know it's probably love

So I push myself away

Thinking I don't deserve you

I tell myself I'm good enough

I wish you'd tell me that too.

Pain is worth more

You promise me forever

All I get is half of you

You want me, you don't

You hurt me with your words.

Damage that you have done

Isn't worth the time I've wasted

My life passes me by

while I'm a pawn in your game

You think I'm sorry wins for you

It only makes me feel less

With every word and every action

My heart gets hurt much more

I was the faithful one while you played your games

Now that I don't chase your heart

You are bitter and show rage

The pain you made me feel

Helped me to feel alive

I found love for someone else

And it happens to be me

The same mistake

A heart so naive,

that betrayal doesn't phase it

Trusting at my mercy

that you could probably change it

There's complexity and beauty

In the smile that I show

But the hidden part of me,

most will never know

Hopeless romantic,

with dreams of a fairytale

They dance in my head

with every lie that he sells

Continuing to see things his way,

because I hope for more
Will he wake up one day
and let his heart open the door?
Will all the attempts to show my heart
Be the ones that makes him see
Why wouldn't he want the same things
Why not just choose me?
Because my love is unselfish
I'll continue to wait for this
For me to be the only one
He'd ever want to kiss
My love shows no boundaries
Because it could never fail
The feelings may fade over time
And time is what will tell.

Maybes

I think about what could've been
The happiness that could ensue

The tears we could've prevented

Had our hearts known what to do

So much pent up aggression

With words left unsaid

For a moment I was alive

Your intentions left me for dead

Our souls entertained the thought

That love could set us free

Pulling away at the last minute

Letting desire leave us be

If there was a way I could tell you

How you stay in my thoughts still

No more what could have beens

It's left up to it'll be what it will.

I could've loved you

With the desire that burns inside

I could've been the faithful one

Until the day that I died.

Instead I get to wait

My heart in your hands

Because I'm not the one you want

Nor what your soul demands.

I'll continue to wait

Until you feel my heart

I'll continue to love from a distance

Until you see my spark.

I wish you could've felt it

The way my heart longed for you

What I was willing to give up

If you could've saw it through.

I would've withstood hell to hold your hand

Gave it all for one moment of us

I miss you everyday but you'd never understand

Because I'm the heart you chose to give up.

Almost

Saddest word in the English language

Counts in certain circumstances

Means more to some

Usually comes without second chances

Almost good enough

He almost loved me

He almost saw me

We almost survived

I almost made it

Broken

One day you will realize

Its me you reach for in the dark

You will search but not find me

You threw me away

You took for granted the love I gave

The things that I did for you

You took advantage of me

And left me for dead

One day you will search

For a heart like mine

You will come up empty

Broken and in the pieces you left me

My memory will softly caress you

Where your spirit needs rest

You will feel the void of me

When you need me the most

You pushed me aside

For affairs of the heart

When you realize what you did

The sorry won't cover it.

The conversation gets shorter

As my emotions fade for you

You miss me, you don't

It's all just a game

The truth is I loved you

But you didn't feel the same

So when you don't find me in the dark

Just know you're the one to blame

Enough?

If I'm not enough

Go find more

If I'm too much

Go find less

Don't come at me with your intentions

Then break me with your words

Don't offer me the world

And just give me dirt

I'm an angel waiting to on my beast

To come tear off my wings

Leave bite marks on my thighs

And make my heart sing

I refuse to lose every part of me

Trying to claim you

Cause my worth is substantial

And your worth is through.

I know I ain't perfect

And you made sure to tell me

Now I'm running away from toxic

My feet can't fail me

What you had

You took for granted

I rolled with the punch you threw

And all the disrespect you handed

Now I'm out here doing me

While you stay texting my phone

Look at you now

Thinking I couldn't be alone

Who you thought you were

Tearing down the realest

Now I'm gonna find my worth

And I promise you'll feel it

You feel like I owe you something

For the damage you created

I'm gonna take back my heart

Since it's the one thing you hated

Go find someone with less

If I'm too much for you

It's a wrap, it's done

Don't be mad cause I'm through

Why not me?

Changes that I notice

When you think I don't

I'd like to tell you I do

But I probably won't

I'll avoid the obvious

And let it consume me

Eating away at my feelings

And I'll just let it be

One minute you want me

The next I don't feel it

It's when I'm doing things for you

When I see your true intent

Miss me with the propaganda

I just want you to be honest

How can I trust you

When you don't give your best?

You act like you want to keep me

But your body says something else

The language that it's showing

Tells me I'm on a shelf

Waiting for the next best thing

That's how I see it

You don't deserve my time

I won't let you receive it

Wishing it could be different

Since we've been something great

But I feel abandoned and used

Thrown away like someone you hate

This could have been beautiful

But you told me what to expect

You cant have even half of me

When I gave you my best

I'm waiting for you

The sting behind the words

You didnt know you said

The sleepless nights after

Replaying it in my head

I see the game you're playing

It makes me feel you less

It won't be long before

I just wish you my best

I give my one hundred

You give me none

I see you for who you are

Guess that means I'm about done

Each time you take from me

The less my heart even needs

You're selfish with your own nature

Leaving my emotions to bleed

It won't be too much longer

And the rest is history

Because I don't hold on to that

And that is my story.

I waited for you to chase me

To even give me half of you

Ive looked for the day

When I was what you'd choose

I don't really have much left

Tired of trying to make it work

Because in the end

I always loved like I'd never been hurt.

Can you just see me?

If you could open your eyes

And see what's in front of your face

You'd see that she's the one for you

And all she has done is chase

She's not perfect by any means

She's damaged and scared to feel

But when you show her you're worthy

She will show you that she is real

Her walls start to fall down

When she finds out she's safe

From that moment on

Your heart will be her place

She will always wonder how you are

And if you need her arms

Will always wonder if you've ate

And if you're warm

She will always dream of you being there

In that place where she's alone

She will want to hold you all night

To make you feel at home

She's a dreamer, head full of ideas

And she will always choose yours first

Stand behind you from day one

Through your best and your worse

Her love is like a diamond

Flawless and rough in texture

But when she loves all of you

Noone can do it better.

He left her broken

He left her broken

Her hurt her heart

He planned to abuse her

From the start

He lured her in

He made her fall

He had no plan

To want it all

Her heart didn't matter

So he let her break

Made her feel unwanted

Left her soul to ache

She tried to hide her pain

Her scars she covered

She held on for so long

While he found another

He regretted what he did

After noone else compared

They couldn't measure up

They didn't even dare

She was one in a million

Her heart was pure and true

Now it's his heart hurting

And he don't know what to do

She refused to be a flower

Picked for her beauty and left to die

She chose to be impossible to forget

Leaving herself wild and difficult to find

You chose her

When I think it's different

I am proved wrong

Over and over again

They never stay long

Glad my heart wasn't in play

Glad I know when to take it out

You almost had it this time

But you made me see without doubt

Give more than I get back

That's the way it goes

Hope it hurts you as much

Cause to me it does

We could've been different

Friends with nothing attached

But feeling emotion with each touch

Was the only catch

I opened my heart to you

And left it vulnerable to pain

Knowing better than to open it

And now I'm to blame

The tears you'll never see

You don't really deserve that

Like you didn't deserve me

Those are the facts

Guess it's on to the next thing

Hope she can replace me

Make sure to love her better

And leave me be

My love is deserving

Of someone that wants me

Not someone that wants no strings

And leaves my heart to bleed

Ghost

He can't see me because I'm a ghost

The conversation left us a long time ago

The hugs and the kisses that once melted a hard exterior

Are a thing of the past.

His ghost reminds me that I was never that important

That I was never more than what I was

It lives in my thoughts and in my heart

But telling him would push him further from me

His ghost still lingers on my lips

As the truth outweighs reality

Because his ghost didn't feel the same

And our souls felt the impact

Living with his ghost is hardest because I felt his soul

Living with mine isn't so hard

Because he didn't feel mine

What you take from me

Taking more than you give

Leaving my heart broken

I should've never let you in

Shouldn't have left myself open

You couldn't even save me

When I needed rescue

All you did was play me

When all I wanted was you

You made time for what you wanted

When all I needed was a friend

You treated me so shitty

My emotions were in the deep end

I couldn't fathom the burden

That I felt I placed on you

But you showed me inconsistent

What else could I do

I wanted a lifetime

With the soul mate I had claimed

You wanted something less

And it made me walk away

You woke up my heart

And built a fire in my soul

Then drown it with your unhappiness

So I have to let you go.

All is fair...or is it

Soulmate

Why can't it be me

Am I not enough

Having a heart like mine

Can sometimes be tough

I wait for that someone

To sweep me off my feet

To dance with me in the dark

To kiss my lips so sweet

Why must I wait for love

To realize that I'm the one?

When is it my turn

To be special to someone?

Why can't he just find me

The soulmate that I claim

So I can feed his soul with mine

And my desire be his flame

My loyalty will be more

Than anything he's ever had

I'll never make him hurt

Not even make him sad

He will walk around with a smile

Because I put it on his face

King of the world

Because I was his saving grace

I'll know him when I see him

Because of how he looks at me

I'll hang his moon and stars

And he'll hang my galaxy.

Let's fall in love

Can we just pretend we're still friends

And make the most of this night

Meet up in a room somewhere private

There's no need to fight it

You can undress me

Piece by piece.

As I breathe in and breathe out

While you use your teeth

I'll caress your skin

My smooth hands charting a path

We can worry about it tomorrow

When we face the aftermath

My hands have longed for you

I'm burning with desire

For a second pretend you love me

Help to extinguish my fire

Your skin could be this paper

Your lips could be this ink

I could finally write a masterpiece

Just from this one link.

Show me your heart

You don't know how loyal I am

Or the way you take my breath

How I would be your everything

Give my all til there's nothing left

Because I daydream of you

And wonder how you are

How sitting beside me in a room

Is still just too far

How I want to hold your hand

And never let you go

How I wish you'd just be real with me

And want to let me know

It's that I feel so infatuated

Everytime we meet up

How it's strange that I fight this feeling

When I know it's probably love

So I push myself away

Thinking I don't deserve you

I tell myself I'm good enough

I wish you'd tell me that too.

Can I?

I just want to binge watch you

And catch up on what I've missed

From the first time I hugged you

To that first time we kissed

I want to explore your mind

See myself in your soul

Learn how to handle your heart

Watch your love unfold

I want to see where your mind takes you

When you're thinking of me

Find out who you think we are

Or what you think we could be

I want to question your instincts

Find the beast within

Feel your untamed passion

And your lips on my skin

I want to know how your heart works

When you hear someone say my name

Find out what you think of me

And if you think I'm a game

I want to know the real you

When noone else is around

What you dream of at night

When you turn the lights down

I want to question your logic

Hoping I can see it too

Want to explain how much I care

And see what I mean to you

I want to dive into your soul

And find me in there

I want to blindly trust your heart

And lay my soul bare

Everything

I wanted to be your everything

I only wanted you

You were not my option

Because I saw your soul

From the moment I kissed you

Until you let me go

You were not my option

Because I put you first

I wouldve crawled through the desert

Just to quench your thirst

I became an option

When there was something else

Now you're my option

Because I already choose myself

I opened that message a thousand times

I couldn't break it to myself

Thinking I could be different

Because of how I felt.

Thinking you'd see me

And who I really was

Someone with alot to give

And still couldn't be enough

I know we made it official

And you told me I wasn't yours

But I gave you the key to my heart

And let you open the door

Who I tried to be for you

I was just playing the fool

Just to try to prove my intentions

I could've been right for you

I'm glad I saw it clearly

It was clear in HD

Who I thought you were

When all you did was play me

I guess I played you too

Cause I agreed to not feel this

But I lied knowing my heart

I knew it from the first kiss.

Hurt is never fair

If you look in my eyes

That's where my demons hide

They show the painful emotions

That I always keep inside

My heart is too kind to show

What my mind keeps saying

My soul is too at peace

To keep up with the game you're playing

I feel like I was your pawn

In a love that didn't last

I was the heart you threw away

And became a part of my past

The memories were absolute

I play them in my head

Wondering what I did wrong

For you to leave my heart for dead

You made sure to remind me

That I wasn't what you wanted

Making sure to hurt me

Leaving me feeling haunted

The damage you did to me

Changed me into someone else

The person I've become

Is a reminder I had nothing left

Let me be free to feel

The happiness I deserve

And I'll figure out how

To forgive the lies I've heard

He don't know her like that

He didn't know her at all

How she wanted but didn't need

How she knew she wasn't the only one

His body language she could read

She always had her doubts

Fell back when she had to ask

Being in her mind

Was always quite the task

Learning his intentions

Started from day one

She knew how she placed

In a game that can't be won

Words don't mean anything

Without action behind them

But she didn't want to question it

For fear of hurting him

She felt part of the game

He was honest from the start

What he didn't account for

Is that she had a heart

He doesn't know she reads him

And is tired of how she tries

It opens her up to quitting

And saying her goodbyes

She's felt like this before

So it's nothing new

If he could only see it

How much she really knew

Her patience, it wore thin

With each time she had to ask

Now asking has became a job

And she's not up for that task

Through tear filled eyes she asked

For one more time with him

But time was too much to give her

Her patience still wearing thin

She realizes what's shes reading

Holds alot of truth

Now what's shes reading

Is that she's done with you

Truth is-I'm done

I hate when you hit me up

I don't answer your calls

I blame me for this one

Cause you're not who I thought

You blame me for the ending

But we didn't always fit

You reminded me of my fault

I didn't deserve that shit

You think you played me

But you showed me the truth

Now I'll show you who I am

And what I can do

You really think I can accept you

For what you've done

When you weren't thinking of me

And now you're not the one

You proved to me a million times

That I wasn't what you want

Now I'll prove a million more

That I can move on

You say you needed a friend

I say find someone new

You won't use me again

Truth is, I only wanted you.

Played out

I hate to think you're playing me

But I dont think you know

From the minute I see you

To the feelings I don't show

The way I hold my breath

Until I see you again

Makes me think it's a phase

A game I'll never win

I tell myself I'm feeling too much

I don't want to push you away

But I think we could make this something

If you really wanted to stay

If you knew how much it hurt

When you talked to me that way

I'll never be able to forget

How it happened that day

I couldn't stand it anymore

You blamed me for what you did

And when I needed to cry

I had to keep it hid

You didnt care that you destroyed me

With all the lies and deception

You only cared that I took care of you

And found your heart where I left it

The pain that I have suffered

Changed me for the worse

My innocence you wasted

Left me with an evil curse

She is...

For her

Being her peace is key

To calming her chaos

Holding her in your arms

And asking how her day was

Her insecurities are from her past

The one she doesn't mention

But making her feel safe

Shows her your intentions

Slowly silencing the voices

Until they fade away

Makes her feel your security

And her feel less afraid

She's a woman inside

Looking for someone like you

When she starts to have trust

Her passions ensue

You'll peel back her layers

To see her inner core

You'll release the clipped wings

And watch your caged bird soar

Loving her is easiest

If you do it with an honest heart

Revealing the girl that you need

She'll show you her best parts.

What if...

What if I'm your ending

And it's the happiest part

What if I was sent to you

To pull you from the dark

What if I'm your comfort

The strength when you're weak

What if I'm your words

When you can't speak

What if I was made for you

And we were meant to be

What if it was fate

And you were made for me

What if this is forever

And you refuse to see

That we are perfect together

Who could we be?

What if you have me all wrong

And use me for your game

When really you were supposed to

Give me your last name

What if you never see

The beauty inside my world

And you still throw me away

And I am never your girl

What if I just walk away

And you don't care to stop me

Because the love I have is worth it

But it's important to set you free

Desire

I'm ready for something better

Something that's meant for me

I dream of something permanent

Wonder who we could be

I wanna feel my value in your presence

Like I'm worth a moment of time

I wanna feel that I am yours

But I want you to be mine

Im waiting on love thats forever

The kind you don't have to ask

I need someone that wants just me

The kind of love that lasts

I don't want to be an option

Not easily replaced

I just want to be happy

And forget the pain I've faced

I can't make you love me

I want you to feel it yourself

Want you to give your heart to me

Not to someone else

I dream of it being you

But if it's not, my heart won't die

Cause you don't deserve my heart

Or the tears that I cry

Hiding my emotions

Because I know you won't believe

That from the beginning

I just wanted you to never leave

I hope...

Someday, it'll be me

When you see me out in a crowd

You'll notice the smile I once gave you

And hear me laugh out loud

I hope you see him kiss me

And you're reminded of the taste

The way my lips were made for yours

It takes you back to that place

I hope he puts his arms around me

The way you used to do

You needed someone else

When all I needed was you

You'll realize how I tried

And gave you the world.

But you treated me like noone

Like I was just another girl

Someday you'll reminisce

About the fun we had

The genuine feeling I gave you

And I hope it hurts you bad

When you see me at that place

Where you and I shared a spark

You'll go home and reach for me

But all you'll see is dark

I hope you remember my smile

And the way I made you laugh

I hope you feel guilty

When you remember the past

When you remember my eyes

And the way you made them cry

Passing me up for someone

Without a reason why

I hope noone compares

And you search for me

When you're laying next to her

Knowing what could be

I hope it burns your throat

Everytime you say my name

When it rolls off your tongue

I hope you know who's to blame

When I needed you most

You left me feeling alone

Sitting next to her

Texting me on your phone

I hope you don't think I was a fool

Cause I chose to ignore the signs

They were just a reminder

You were never really mine.

I hope you never come across another

With a heart as good as mine

And when you're ready to fall in love

I hope it's something you don't find

Her

She's just like water

Powerful enough to drown you

Her strength you can feel

If you only knew

She's soft enough to cleanse you

Of all the pain you've had to feel

She's wholehearted and loving

Her touch makes you feel real

She's deep enough to save you

From the demons in your mind

True woman in every aspect

Best you'll ever find

She's wet enough to savor

Freak down to her core

When you leave from her side

You'll want to come back for more

She's warm enough for you to hold

Her hugs remind you of home

She'll never make you feel pain

Will never make you feel alone

She's cold enough to have your back

When the streets are not that kind

She'll stand to fight with you

Never leave you behind.

She's hot enough to burn you

Like her temps 200 degrees

She'll make you feel desired

By begging for you on her knees

She gentle enough to love you

This Queen that is so rare

A diamond in the rough

Just waiting for you to care.

Emotions of love

I've wasted a whole lifetime

Learning to love myself

Even killing my emotions

Placing my heart on a shelf

Smiling while dying

Intuition is a gift

Its tough seeing the future alone

I'll stay in ignorant bliss

Feeling that I deserve the world

And someone willing to share

Why can't they see the real me

Or at least act like they care

Going hard for love that lasts

Twisted behind my heart

Sometimes feeling I'm not worth it

Not the time or the respect, not one part

Just waiting for that one person

To tell me I'm never alone

Someone to fill the blank space

A place to call home

Friends to entertain passion

It's sometimes hard to fathom

Can't you see that I'm more

I just don't understand it

Silently I suffer

Alone in the dark at night

I'm not saying that I'll find it

But I'm saying that I might

Steadfast and motivated

To make positive change

If you don't see all of me

Guess you're the one to blame

Proudly complex, a whole person

I love with everything I have

Show me you're worth my effort

Would that be so bad?

Butterfly

I'm changing like a butterfly

My cocoon is almost empty

I've spread my wings to fly away

All behind what you did to me

You opened my heart

So I could love you just enough

Then put me on my knees

Just to beg for your touch

Forget you and all your games

I finally found my strength

No more jumping through hoops

Or going through great lengths

Instead I'll fly away

Leaving you stranded

I won't let you take my heart

Or my life for granted

I'll let you keep the memories

Though I wish I could erase them

Instead I'll erase them from my mind

Cause I don't really need em

Change my number or my name

Nah, you're not worth it

Point fingers or take blame

None of it was certain

I'll let you go do you

And I'll continue to be me

Letting go will be hard

But it's you that set me free

His other half

So much more

Than Just a ride or die

I'll get your back

Take the wheel and drive

I'll be your protector

Be your other eye

I'll stand with you

When the world ain't on your side

I'll climb any mountain

Any hill you can climb

Swim across any sea

Just to call you mine

Support your dreams

Though they're not my own

Hold you up

When everyone else lets you down

Cater to you like a king

Rub your back and neck

Treat you like my number one

Give no disrespect

I'll be your other gun

Cause you're my other half

I'd give you the world

And all that I have.

Women like me

Women like me...

We act like we don't need anyone

But when I curl up by myself

I wish there was someone.

Girls like me...

We know what pain is

It was given at the hands of the one

That we once trusted

People like me...

We fear for our heart

It's easily manipulated when given away

And thats the hardest part

Hearts like mine...

They love with no regrets

How else would it see beauty

In everyone it met

Love like mine....

It's kind and trusting

You get what you see

It cant wait for someone to love me

Souls like mine...

Have been looking for someone like you

But hearts like yours,

Refuse to see my heart too.

She is woman

When she walks in

Chaos ensues

Her style, her grace, the way she walks

The room thanks itself for her existence

She's not your typical woman

She's got what they don't

Courage, bravery, strength

When she should just give up

How dare a man to use her

Like she's a revolving door

When she opens up to you

Lock the door and throw away the key

She builds homes out of tents

Cooks meals from nothing

She is woman, the real thing

You'll never replace her

Others have tried to be her

They've failed to steal her shine

They tried to break her

But, that girl could smile.

Just when you think you know her

She will surprise you with her heart

And when you think she's like everyone else

She's different, so much different

Every opportunity to love her

Has been wasted on boys

But in the hands of the right man

Lord can she fly

She'd take all those pieces of rust

That are inside your soul

And turn them into gold

If you'd only let her

Knowing her is amazing

This beautiful friend of mine

And when I say it's been my pleasure

I mean that in every way possible

She's the kind of fire

That you burn with

Not the kind

You play with

Her heart

You wanna know my heart

And the way to get it

It doesn't come easy

I have to admit

I won't jump into love

Until you show me it's safe to fall

I won't make you love me

If you don't want it all

I'll check on you if you're mine

To make sure you're okay

I'll cuddle you on the couch

When you've had a long day

I'll wrap my legs around you

When we sleep at night

I won't tell you I love you

Even though I might

I'll treat your soul like paper

Careful not to tear it apart

I'll hold your feelings close to me

And keep you in my heart

I'll make each day an adventure

With laughter and fun to share

You'll never have to wonder

If I really care

I'll tell you your value to me

You'll always know your worth

Cause when you're mine

I'll always make you first

I won't make this complicated

If you really need to know

To have my heart is easy

Just don't ever wanna let go

Just a girl

The girl who's always there

Always ends up alone

She is your safe place

And makes you feel at home

She loves with a generous heart

But deep down she's scarred

Why does she feel this way

When she tries so hard

They use her body for pleasure

And she lets them for fun

Maybe someday they'll see her

And choose her as the one

Damage that they've caused

Has taken over her soul

She cries when she's alone

When she has to see them go

She just wants someone to stay

That doesn't want to leave

Someone that knows a woman's worth

And can make her believe

She'd give her heart completely

If given the right chance

But noone sees her inner soul

Not even a second glance

Her life isn't always fair

The pieces she puts back together

Will she even find tru love

Or someone that wants forever

So she prays for a miracle

In this game of love and war

As she searches for who she is

And the one she was made for

The girl that's always there

Is starting to find herself

She'll leave it all behind

And they'll all have nothing left

She is me

She's complicated, a little shy

She loves hard and falls harder

She's a flower in the garden

Waiting for the sun to shine

She gives more of herself

Than she ever gets in return

The one thing she wants the most

Is unreachable and can't be found

She continues to search for true love

The kind that doesn't waiver

The person that hungers for her smile

The one she can't live without

Loving her is like breathing

She makes sense of chaos

But who will ever know that

Because her layers are so deep

She's a queen in every way

Though truth and honesty she seeks

She's waiting on love that's honest and true

She may never find it is a reality

She'd sweep you off your feet

If you gave her the permission

She'd be the best she could be

And be faithful and honest.

She is me, I am complicated

I love hard and fall harder

I could be the one if given the chance

I love hard because I know how it feels to be loved so little

What I need

I dont need someone to stitch me together

I need someone to let me know it's okay to bleed

I don't need someone to open my heart

Just to fill their need

I need someone strong enough

To love me at my worse

With a heart so loyal to me

That he lets me know my worth

I need a soldier of war

To fight my past and win

To never give up on me

Even if I do again and again

I need some understanding

That I'm complex and rare

A diamond that's undiscovered

By someone that didn't care

I need someone dignified

So they can show me the truth

Someone that isn't scared of how much I am

Someone that will see it through

I need someone with two hands

One for each side will suffice

One for the naughty side

One for the nice

I need a musician

To fill my world with lyrics

Just enough for me

Noone else has to hear it

I need a lion that roars

And makes me purr along

To the sound of his voice

So I can sing his song

I need someone that isn't scared

Of the fact that love has been unkind

That my heart has been too much for everyone

And what I've searched for I can't find

More than anything...

I need someone to dance me around the kitchen

At 2 am while making a snack

Or holds me when I cry

And always has my back

I need him to want a ride or die

That's got it together

I need him to know

That I want his forever.

I don't need him to be scared of me

Or the fact that I am real

I just need someone that won't give up on love

And is true to what he feels

I need him to be honest

And tell me what I mean

To let me know the truth

With no in between

I need him to want to wake up to me

Messy hair and all

But I want to curl up with him at night

Into his arms I fall

I want his whole heart

I won't settle for less

And if I can't have it

I'll try to give him my best

If he can't see that I'm the truth

And my love for him is pure

Hopefully I'll see the truth

And won't love him anymore

Cruel world

In a world that's cruel

She understood why it was

They couldn't figure out

Why she stayed so much above

Her heart was too kind

To hurt anyone else

She hid her pain

Until she learned to love herself.

As free as a bird

That had always been caged

Soaring above the clouds

Hoping he sees the change

Wishing he would realize

That she is all he needs

Wishing she could wake up his heart

Just to see how hers bleeds

If her eyes could tell her story

The inventory they hold

Full of pain and regret

But still loves to her soul

Hopeless romantic

In love with the thought

It don't have to be material

She didn't want what could be bought

Self Reflection

Self reflection is the mission

In my story to tell

All of the things that I hide

I know me so well.

I have autumn in my eyes

They are blue like the sky

They hide my indiscretions

The color blue when I cry

From my heart,

most everyone runs

It's huge and gets broken easy

It can burn you like the sun

Love is all we really need

I want it all

I don't want temporary

I want permanent

I want the good days

I want the bad days

I want the days when u wake up

And you can't stand me

I want the days when u are at your worse

And I'm the only safe haven u have

I want your best days

I want the laughs and cuddles

I want pillow fights on Sunday morning

I want to make you breakfast in bed

I want good night kisses

Slow dancing in the kitchen

I want to know the places that hurt

I want to know how to take it away

I want to kiss away your tears

I want to have your back

I want you to know who I am

I want you to have my heart

More than anything

I want years, not months

I want love, not lust

I want you to feel good in my presence

I want you to miss me like I do you

I want you to think of me everyday

I want to be the first call you make

And the last prayer at night.

I want permanent. Not temporary

Safe with me

You are the inspiration

Behind all of my writing

The wild thoughts

In my head each day

The golden path of stars

That light my heart

The reason I smile each morning

The peace to my chaos

The laugh behind my smile

The bandaid to my wound

You are the soul

That my heart needs to feel

The touch that my takes me

To a place I've never been

The only person that makes me climax

Over and over again

If your body is a map

Let me explore you

Because my body is yours

To pleasure you beyond your wildest dreams

This has became magic

Your art is my muse

Everyday is an adventure

That I never want to end

I see you in my dreams

I feel you in my soul

Your heart is safe with me

I don't want to let you go

How it feels

They don't understand how it is

To be a woman that is hidden

Good enough for sex

Conversation seems necessity

Each hotel key hurts more

Each time he has to leave

Seems the persistence to go

Gets greater after each link

I know my worth and that it's no good

But I keep waiting to feel what's not there

Good enough to fuck

Hidden from the world

One day I'll find my worth

And I'll change my vision

He won't hurt me that bad

And my heart will heal

Hoping he will someday see that I'm enough

But knowing I'll never be

Good enough to sex

Not enough to take out

Each passing day is a reminder

That I'm better than that

Still I hunger

For the touch of his hand

When I find my worth

I'll leave him alone

And I won't feel so alone

When he don't call

I know he's out there

The one that thinks I'm worth it

He will have me on his arm

And show the world I'm his

Love

The love I have is real

If you ever wanted to know

I'd make you laugh through tears

Just to dry up your emotions

I'd eat through all of your pain

So you wouldn't have to swallow it

I'd hold you up if you fell

To help you find strength

I'd hold you down through bad times

And celebrate all of the good

Id make love to your mind

And let your body follow

I'd worship your beautiful lips

And hug away your fears

I'd make you see your beauty

In a world full of ugly

You don't know that you're mine

And I plan to make you see that

Because my plans for you

Go beyond lust or sex

You can fall into my heart

And I'll swim through your soul

We will find a commonplace to meet

Where our eyes will lock in love

Our souls will intertwine with the touch of a hand

And you'll know what love sounds like

By the beat of my heart, you'll hear it

From across the room

Kiss me

I need him to kiss me good morning

Like I was the reason the sun decided to shine

I need him to touch my body

Like his fingers would die without it

I need him to look at me like he'd go blind

I need him to taste me like I'm his favorite drink

If hes going to love me, he needs to be solid.

With eyes for only me and a heart that's unchanged

Because how terrible is it to be called smart and beautiful

But still be alone every night

Don't approach a woman's heart

If you don't have intentions to love her

Don't make her think she's all you need

If she's not all that you want.

His head on my chest while he breathes in and out

I wonder if he can hear my heart saying

You're home.

Love

The love I have is real

If you ever wanted to know

I'd make you laugh through tears

Just to dry up your emotions

I'd eat through all of your pain

So you wouldn't have to swallow it

I'd hold you up if you fell

To help you find strength

I'd hold you down through bad times

And celebrate all of the good

Id make love to your mind

And let your body follow

I'd worship your beautiful lips

And hug away your fears

I'd make you see your beauty

In a world full of ugly

You don't know that you're mine

And I plan to make you see that

Because my plans for you

Go beyond lust or sex

You can fall into my heart

And I'll swim through your soul

We will find a commonplace to meet

Where our eyes will lock in love

Our souls will intertwine with the touch of a hand

And you'll know what love sounds like

By the beat of my heart, you'll hear it

From across the room

He is home

He felt warm and familiar

Solid and safe

I wanted to cling to his shirt

Bury my face in his neck and never let go

I could breathe in his presence

The air around him intoxicating

Loving him was like oxygen

When I needed to live

I had to be in his presence

It didn't matter how it happened

I needed to hear his laugh

I didn't care if it was not for me

I could taste him on my tongue

After every sweet kiss

Couldn't get him outta my head

After Everytime we met

The voice of reason told me to hold my emotions aside

But the minute he touched me

All that doubt faded away

For one more scent of him

I'd give up everything

For one more day with him

I'd die a thousand deaths

There's no doubt where I left my heart

Because I don't possess that anymore

He gave me just enough to love him

But pulled it away when I needed it.

He handcuffed me in poetry

His tongue was the pen

His hands were the paper

He turned me into his art

Loyalty

Give me loyalty

Love can be overrated

I don't need your love

No reason for me to explain it

If he could be loyal

I wouldn't be alone

All the sleepless nights

I stare at the ceiling in our home

The late night phone calls

I know he didnt miss

The times he said I was crazy

Wasted time on just his kiss

Being alone wasn't worth

The pain I had to feel

Being alone now is different

It's when the pain seems too real

Come back to me he cried

And you will never feel that again

I wouldn't have felt it

If he would've loved me in the beginning

Had the lies cut his throat

Each time he told them

Had the betrayal been a knife

My scars would be from him

My strength comes in waves

When I'm at my lowest

He hates who I've become

Took him long enough to notice

My loyalty didn't matter

As long as I paved the way

His loyalty left me shattered

He replaced me everyday

Time wasted

I refuse to beg anymore

For any of your time

Valuable precious minutes

You wasted of mine

I felt like I gave you me

But you didn't even set you aside

The more I had to beg

The more my feelings died

Maybe you were afraid to be honest

For fear of making me cry

But all you had to do was tell me

So I didn't continue to try

Wasted time and wasted money

Two things I hated the most

You didn't even break me

My feelings were never your loss

Instead it woke me up

That I could be so vulnerable

Back inside my heart goes

Lesson learned, I'm insufferable

What you didn't know

I play this game well

With every sign you threw

Every story you tell

In not new to this at all

I've played my part too

Only problem is you played me

I didn't play you

Friendships that last a lifetime

Partners in crime

Partners in crime

Has a good ring

He's mine and I'm his

We've made this a thing

Our energy we match

We know that's the vibe

No pressure, no expectations

Just along for the ride

We laugh, we have fun

We just get each other

Time seems to disappear

When we're together

Discreet and to the point

No judgement, no lies

I like the way he laughs

He likes my thick thighs

Partners in crime

We play our positions

We ride or die

Like it's our only mission

For My Jerry

A friendship unmatched

We vibe on a different level

The laughter is undeniable

When we're together

We throw punches and eat

I'm digging his style

I always got his back

I'd go the extra mile

We've been so inseparable

Since the beginning of forever

Always stay in touch

When we're not together

He understands who I am

Even when I don't

He makes me see clearly

Even when I won't.

His judgement is non existent

He redeems who we are

He's my rock in tough times

I'm his bright shining star

Brother to the end

He's always there for me

Always present in the moment

No other place I'd rather be

Supporting and loyal

He has never let me down

He always makes me smile

Even when I wanna be down

I'd ride out for him

This true friend of mine

Nothing has kept us apart

Not distance or time.

Just Friends?

A friendship made by chance

That seems to fit just right

Because he gets in my head

And stays there all night

The thought of his lips

When they kiss me like that

Makes my soul start a fire

He hands me the match

He hugs me with passion

I don't want him to let go

I feel safe in his embrace

I want to let him know

I'm scared that he will think

That for him I am obsessed

But it sure does feel like home

When my head is on his chest

The way he makes me love

The things I hate about myself

He wakes up a broken heart

That I placed on a shelf

With hands that repair the cracks

In my imperfect soul

He touches me in places

Noone else would ever go

His eyes seem to devour me

With a look of pure desire

When he stares into my eyes

It sets my body on fire

He allows me to explore him

Like an undiscovered treasure

Under my impatient hands

Is where I give him pleasure

My lips can't wait to kiss him

Tongue ready to taste his skin

When I am in his presence

I can't hide my mischievous grin

His laughter takes over

And makes my heart feel light

Taking all of my senses

To a completely different height

Profane bliss

You're mine

My mind is full of dirty thoughts

I shouldn't think this way

I just want you to say to me

Baby it's time to play

I want you to bite my thighs

To put your hand around my throat

To overpower me like I'm yours

To overpower my mouth until I choke

I want your mark on me

Use your hands to leave it there

I want you to forget your respect

And act like you don't care

I want your disrespect

Treat me like I'm your whore

Own me like I'm your property

Make me beg for more

Dirty thoughts fill my head

While you fill my body

Say all those dirty things to me

Make me submit and be naughty

I'm yours for a moment

Suspended in profanity and bliss

Who knew that your sex

Could ever feel like this.

Tie me up with your passion

Your tongue igniting my flame

If I don't surrender to you

Make me the one to blame

Take out your frustrations on me

While your power takes control

Let your lips linger on me

Take possession of my soul

Mindfuck me with your words

Turn me on with your smile

Whisper what you want from me

My body's yours to defile

Spread your seed all over me

As you make me moan for you

This pussy is yours for the taking

The lust I can't undo

The thoughts, they make me wet

Everytime I think of you

I crave your sweet taste

Your body knows what to do

I'll suck out your soul

And swallow what comes

Make me taste your juices

Until you're satisfied and done

I'll bottle up those moments

When we play our little game

Make me want you again

Make me say your name

Passionate

His hands on my flesh

They burn me with fire

His lips on my lips

They cure my desire

The way he handles my body

Like its his personal possession

The way his eyes burn to my soul

Like I'm his one obsession

When he enters inside me

It's the cure for my anxiety

When he puts his arms around me

There's no other place I'd rather be

I know he don't belong to me

He's not mine to claim

But I do know I wouldn't mind

If he was the candle and I, his flame

We don't label what is there

There are things left unsaid

He stays in my heart daily

But more, he stays in my head

The thoughts they spin around

On a merry go round of intensity

Looking for a sign of life

Praying that he can't see

Breathing his thoughts in

While masking the burn

Not making it part of a game

My passion is his to learn

Someday becomes everyday

And the heat burns hidden desire

If he touches me when we meet

My skin will catch on fire

Hiding my eyes behind my heart

Cause it's like today's fashion

I wear it on my sleeve

Because he's my one passion

He knows who he is

The taste of your skin

The sound of your sigh

I know that it feels good

I also know why

The sound of your breathing

It gets heavier as I approach

The climax that you long for

Happens with my gentle touch

I miss you before you're gone

But those feelings I don't show

I fear you'll run away

If I were to let you know

The way you embrace me

Like I'm the one for you

I try to hide my heart

Because I don't know what to do

We arranged no strings

But my heart has been tied

I tell myself I can do this

But my soul tells me I lied

If you knew the way I feel you

As if you're a part of my skin

Please let him see me

And want to hold me again

I run from the feeling you give

I'm scared you don't feel me

I tell myself I'll suppress it

Please don't let him see

He's the muse to my poetry

But my feelings are left unsaid

How can I get him out of my heart

When I can't even get him outta my head?

Savored moments

From the moment he kissed me

My lips burned like a flame

I had no idea his toxicity

Would burn my heart too

He was my song and his heart my lyrics

There were some things in this world that were too lovely for words

He was one of them

He ignited my passion with a fire that wouldn't cease

His soul was a masterpiece built of pain and love

Rolled into one, he was complex and mysterious

I peeled his layers and found more than I had sought after

He was the closest that I had been to home

His touch was my house

The peace I'd longed for

If passion and love could have saved us

There was plenty to spare

But despair and pain covered us

Until we felt no more

How I wish it could've lasted

When he walked in the room

His scent captivated me

His eyes shining bright with flecks of excitement

He's the one I've been waiting for

This wasn't supposed to happen like this

But his body made me comfortable

Every single kiss let me know that he wanted me

His body language let me know he's feeling the same

Strangers can't fall this hard

without consequence

But I fell this hard

without circumstance

He doesnt know how toxic he is

But I'll try to stop the thoughts

Because kissing him is like breathing

And his oxygen is all that I want.

Sex is a weapon

You say you love me

But I don't feel it

You say our souls are embedded

Like lovers intertwined in a kiss

You say I'm the one for you

When you leave I lose connection

The words you use to pursue me

Prove that I'm just a destination

Putting my heart on my sleeve

Makes me vulnerable to you

I hide my true feelings

Because you don't reciprocate

I could've loved you for more than sex

But you throw me away when it's over

It takes away pieces of me

When you use my body so well

I wish I could tell you how I feel

Running you away scares me

I know you're no good for me

And you may never want more

Your sex is a weapon

And you use it so well

It's been my pleasure

Hugging him is like home

The comfort in his embrace

His domination is comforting

It's sometimes my saving grace

The burn of his passion

When his hands are on my skin

In blissful wonder I'm thinking

Where has he always been

The wild dirty thoughts

That race my mind everyday

Always desiring for more

When he needs me to come play

He doesn't know how loyal I am

To the feelings that burn for him

I just know that it's a hot white flame

That I hope never goes dim

Enjoying every stolen moment

When I catch a glimpse of his eyes

Every minute anticipating

Because his limit is the sky

Tangled up in sexual passion

When two people unite as one

I hold onto his body

To feel him quiver when I'm done

My role is his pleasure

And I play my part so well

His role is my dominant

That role he's never failed.

The way he makes me feel

It's when he pulls me close

And whispers in my ear

"I've been craving you all day"

Only for me to hear

It's when he makes that noise

The one that's just for me

That low gutteral laughter

It almost sets me free

It's when he kisses my thigh

While I please him with my throat

The feel of him on my skin

While his manhood makes me choke

It's when he tells me I'm his

His claim to me is real

It opens a level of wetness

Only he's allowed to feel

It's when he says he needs it

Like its his favorite part

If he knew I needed it more

But I'm too shy to start

It's when he isn't afraid

Of how much I really am

A woman with no boundaries

Who loves to pleasure that man

It's when I'm driving home

When my legs stop shaking

If he only knew

I'm his for the taking

Discreet

Take my message from your phone

Don't let them see what we do

This should only be a relationship

That's kept between us two

Electric sex that fails to judge

We fantasize the moment

Our bodies crave the passion

It makes us want it

I yearn to touch your body

It speaks to me

A language of desire

That always sets me free

Give me what I need

But if I must, I'll beg you

Your touch is what I long for

It's always long overdue

Don't tell em about us

Let's keep this discreet

You give me what I want

I'll be what you need

Kiss and tell, that's not me

I don't brag on what we have

I won't judge you for your fetish

You don't judge me for my past

Kiss me in words unspoken

Let me put you on my tongue

The way you caress my body

Is what I'm hung up on

Let's do this with no limit

See how far we can go

I promise that I'm worth it

Press play, let's go.

Take my breath away

Breathe fire into me

As you breathe on my neck

I anticipate what's going to happen

I can't wait for what's next

Silencing my voices

So they don't tell me no

But with each brush of your fingers

I just have to know

Melting into you

You know just what to do

To make my mind scatter

Until all I think of is you

You slowly touch my back

It takes my breath away

For a minute I forget to breathe

While you continue to play

Please don't look in my eyes

They tell you I want more

You do things to me

Like no man before

Lyrics for him

Sometimes I fall back

But I can't get enough of you

With a body so sexy

Baby can I come taste you

Everytime they see us out

They tryna holla

You don't sweat these girls

You know I'm your balla

Only one with stamina

We can go all night

Go hard or go home

We steady with the fight

When you know it ain't easy

It must be real If you deserve it

Turning my head ain't gon be easy

Show me that you worth it

Good love don't come free

The rest may not deserve it

Let's see how far this goes

Show me you gon be worth it

Hit hard and go deep

Ass so fat for my baby

Thinkin bout it the day after

Can you call me back, maybe

Get in looking so good

I keep it clean for that man

Cause he hit home runs in the majors

Noone can do it like he can

Sexin til the morning

Put this phat cat on your plate

Hurry up and pull up

Boy don't be late

Hit it from the top

Let me look in your eyes

Let me drown you tonight

While u drip down my thighs

I'm loyal and I'm patient

I got eyes only for you

Baby let me come taste you

Tell me to come through.

Wild thoughts

My mind has filthy thoughts

I don't really care to share

I'm scared of what they'll say

If I'd only dare

I learned to love myself

Even my thick thighs

The one part that I hate

Horrible through my eyes

Spend my time surrounded

By people everywhere

But always dreaming

Of the one I wish was there

He loves me with no reason

Can't wait to feel my touch

He is patient and kind

I'm never too much

He devours my body

Like it belongs to him

For a moment we're one

Passion shines, we never let it dim

Fantasies

Erotic fantasies when we meet

I try to hide my desire

The whole time we're talking

My womanhood is on fire

The sound of your voice

When you're near

I want to fuck you hard

Whispering in my ear

I touch your thighs

Thinking of how they'd feel

If I could just kiss them

My fantasy is much too real

Your hands when I see them

I can feel them touch me there

The way they explore my sexuality

You hold me like you care

I want to beg you to touch me

Caress my skin with your hands

No one has ever touched my soul

Can't do it like you can

The good part

There were parts of her

That had never been touched

She had never been enough

Or told she was too much

He came along and touched her

She could feel him in her skin

She knew she'd never felt this

Only when she's with him

His white hot touch

Flames burning red

He stayed in her thoughts

Remained in her head

The heat from his passion

Took her breath away

For once she felt beautiful

From that first day

He looked like he could devour her

Her lips quivered when they met

She knew how much she wanted him

His body, soul and spirit.

Her desire for him lit her flame

Sexual desire made her burn

He made her feel sexy

His desire she had to earn

When she finally felt him

Her heart pounded with desire

He was the flame she couldn't put out

He lit her soul on fire.

She wants much more

Than just to touch him again

She wants him to leave his mark

On every inch of her skin

Let's roll together

Come waste my time

Come waste some time with me

Cause I need to feel your touch

We don't have to be together

You don't have to say you're in love

Come spend some time alone

Lets break these transgressions

Take it all out on me

Show me your aggression

Come see who I really am

Cause that's who I don't show

Play your part just right

Nobody has to know

Come get to know the real me

The one who I can't show

See if we have a vibe

Let's make this rythym flow

Come take a break with me

If I'm even worth your time

I don't have to be yours

I wont call you mine

Come sleep the night away

My head laid on your chest

Just know I've gave everything

I've always tried the hardest

Come waste the day away

This may be the last time

It won't take long to realize

That you're not mine.

I will find you

Let me show you what you're missing

Come talk to me a while

All I wanted was to hug you

Make you laugh and see you smile

My intentions got the best of me

Cause I thought you were worth it

But your intentions weren't the same

You didn't think I deserved it

I could've showed you love

No judgement, just real

My heart was just too loyal

To what I wanted to feel

I let you use me up

While falling deep in love

But Everytime I left you

I felt not good enough

But the games not always a loss

Cause I saw right through

Now I'm the one that's winning

I'm better because of you

I'm motivated to find him

This soulmate that I seek

He will love with no limits

And only want me.

Let's go today

Would you wanna roll with me?

Can you catch my vibe?

Would you wanna lay with me

Could you stay the night?

Could I wake up next to you

Feel your body on my skin

Press my face into your chest

Kiss you on your chin

Would you just tell me no

Because you don't feel it too

Or could you forget about me

Like I can't forget about you

Could you put your arms around me

Your lips heavy against mine

Kiss me madly and deeply

Take my breath away each time

Could you stroke my thighs

Linger there for a while

Make me feel like a woman

Because you make me smile

Place your body on my tongue

You know what I intend

I know where this goes

Cause I love the end

Let's tangle up in my sheets

Let your body relax in my bed

It should always be this way

When you're in my head

Pull up on me

Come catch a vibe with me

Let me lay on your chest

Get the scent of my hair

While I listen to your breath

Stay for hours, don't wanna leave

Let me feel who you are

Your kisses are like bourbon

They burn my throat with fire

The way you say my name

It sounds so sexy

I don't know what it is

But somehow you just get me

Catch the way I look at you

Like you're my favorite flavor

The taste of you on my lips

Is something that I savor

I hope you feel our vibe

Like I feel you

Anytime you want me

I'll come through

Just know I'm at your request

Anytime you want me

When you need a refill

You know who to come see

Are you down?

Come ride with me

In the city with lights that glow

Let's roll the windows down

And let our hair blow

Come get a little closer

Let's see where this goes

Scoot close to me in the seat

Let's pretend noone knows

Come look in my eyes

Let me see you smile

We will drive for hours

Maybe a hundred miles

Come beat the streets with me

Let's get to know each other

You tell me how you want me

And I'll be your lover

Come slide into my seat

Let's pass the night away

You don't gotta come home with me

I won't make you stay

Come catch this cool breeze

While your scent blows around

I'll hang onto every word

Just let me know you're down

Come drive me through the lights

Let's make this our time

You can pretend that I'm yours

Can I call you mine?

For my twinflame

Where have you been?

She spends her time alone

Wondering why she is

She's complex, beautiful, whole

But she's still not enough

She's realizing what she's worth

Wondering when someone else will

Where's her prince? The one?

Where's her forever?

Everyday she tries so hard

To be who he needs

Everyday, she feels more alone

Wondering when it's her turn

She just wants the one

That misses her smile

That wants to see what she's wearing

That wants her attention

Sure he misses her

Or that's what he feeds her

But the same energy

Can't seem to form a call

Still she stays vigilant

Hoping one day she's worth it

The work she puts in

Will it ever reciprocate ?

The time she's spent on her knees

Will now be spent on her feet

Running from what hurts

And toward what she wants

Tired of waiting for him

She loves herself more each day

Realizing she may never find it

Knowing that love is a forgotten word

It will always be you

I don't need his money

I don't need his cars

Forget all that paper

I just want his heart

He chases the fortune

While I chase his soul

He dont let me catch him

It makes me wanna let go

The chase has been exhausting

Years in the making

I'd dead them all for him

To keep his heart from breaking

My soulmate undercover

The one I dream about

He'd never need anyone else

I'd love him without a doubt

Intimidating I can be

I dream in vivid color

He sees in black and white

My distant hopeless lover

For one chance to prove

That I'm everything he needs

I'd never break his heart

Begging on my knees

If he could see what I see

The passion he would feel

If he'd peek inside my heart

He'd know my love is real

Patiently waiting for him

To come claim this forever

It's been a long wait

For us to be together

Cupid will shoot his arrow

This time he won't miss

And in love I'll fall

With just one kiss.

When will you need me?

When was the last time

I told you how special you are

How my arms wish they could hold you

Across the room from you is still too far

How my lips long for your kiss

Even when I just kissed you

How my legs want to feel your touch

Each stroke of your hand feels brand new

How I daydream about your eyes

When you're smiling at me

They make me feel alive

And wanna be who you need

How my hair wants you to play in it

To feel you soothe my soul

How warm I feel in your embrace

I don't want to let you go

How my feet want to run through your mind

And stay there all day

How I can't wait to talk to you

To hear what you have to say

When was the last time you heard

That you're an amazing soul.

When was the last time I said

Please don't let me go

When you weren't looking

When you weren't looking

I smiled at your laugh

When you weren't watching

I thought about my past

When you didn't see it

My stomach dropped to my feet

When you didn't feel it

My heart skipped a beat

When you didn't pay attention

I cried for the last time

When you didn't want me

I wanted you to be mine

When you didn't talk to me

I became stronger

When you didn't listen to me

I didnt hold on any longer

When you thought you had me

I slowly pulled away

When you didn't miss me

I didn't want to stay

When you thought you knew me

I was gone like the wind

Cause what you thought I didn't know

Was the reason for the end

He's it

His love is like breathing

I need him like oxygen

I need his arms to hold me

His hands to touch me again

I need to breathe him in

And drown in his kiss

I need him to be in my head

And dream of his passionate bliss

I need to hear his voice

Without it I won't survive

Because the way he says my name

Is what keeps me alive

The scent of him when he leaves

Is more than I can stand

This isn't just love that I feel

Its deeper than the ocean

I want him like he's a drug

That I can't come down from

I want to be in his presence

Until I can't get enough

I don't know what he did to me

To wake up my broken heart

I do know that it's amazing

And I don't want to lose that part

If forever exists, it's him

He's what I need him to be

He unlocked the door to my heart

And I've given him the keys

For him

There are 7 billion hearts

In the world around tonight

His is the only one

That I want to put ahead of mine

I'll hold his heart in my hands

Without fear that it will hurt

Because when he is inside me

I just want to make it work

If he would collapse into me

He'd never have to fall again

I'd fall right into his arms

All he has to do is say when

I wake up everyday knowing

He's the adventure I want

The rest of my life isn't enough

Just say you love me, you don't have to front

I just want to fall asleep

In his mind, his body, his soul

Tangled up with each other

Let's see how far this goes

May my heart

Be the softest place he falls

And my soul

Be the wildest place he runs

Because of him

Why do I open myself like this

But only open for him

He's the stars in the sky

Pushing through the clouds in my soul

He's rain, on a hot summer day

When the heat is hard to bear

When each breath takes strength

He's the oxygen that gives me life

He's the warmth of a blanket

When winter is bitter and cold

He's like a fire to my body

When I've been cold my entire life

He don't know the inspiration

The trail of smiles he leaves with me

The strength from each laugh

The silent poetry that fills my heart

On the hardest days, I don't have to pretend

On the easy ones, he makes me shine

All of the power exchanges in his presence

And the rest of the world fades into the background.

He is my inspiration

He is the sun, when the rain is too heavy

The warmth on my face that gives me a glow

The weakness I feel when my heart is the strongest

When he comes around the corner

My heart skips a beat

I try to hide my emotions because I know they're not returned

Hoping for a change in mind that still may never come

But still believing that our souls

Will intertwine on another level

His sensitive side makes me weak

While his dominant side makes me wet

The hunger for his arms wrapped around me

Is almost more than I can stand

I feel like I'm an option in the game he plays so well

I take my heart out of play so it doesn't shatter in the moment

He is the sun that breaks through the clouds of my soul

If only I could tell him how inspiring- he is.

Waiting

I spend my days waiting, for that one phone call

It tells me that you can't be without me

You ask me to be yours forever and never spend another night alone

I ask you to be my forever

Waiting on a dream that I've held for so long

Because I see the potential in you

I see a beautiful person full of strength

But damaged behind the scenes.

I wait for different outcomes

I know may never come true

You don't discuss your feelings

It's left in the air by you

Please tell me where we stand

I get tired of guessing

It's only your intentions

That I wish to question

If you would just let me know

That I have the opportunity for love

I'd handle your heart fragilly

Like a pair of white gloves

Jealous

The way everyone gets to be in your presence

The time they get to spend watching you smile

The other people that get to enjoy you

The limits I have on time

The shirt you wear that hugs your body

The belt that gets to buckle around your waist

The shoes that get to be worn on your feet

The way my hands wish that I could hold you like they do

The pillow that you hold tight when you sleep

The water that gets to hydrate your body

I'm jealous of the wine you drink

To soothe your tired mind

I'm jealous of the things that know you more than I

The things that you need to survive throughout the day

Wishing I could be in that world

So I could be part of that

I'm jealous that I'm not needed

To fulfill your daily tasks

That my oxygen isn't the thing that you need

That my heartbeat isn't what keeps you moving

I'm jealous of the sun that shines on your face

When you turn your eyes to see it

I'm jealous of everything that knows about you

Because I still have to learn.

I dream of him

Dreaming in color

Of love that lasts

It doesnt judge my present

Doesn't linger in the past

Dreaming of him

Leaving me breathless

I know who he is

His soul is relentless..

Dreaming to find him

I know he's out there

He holds my heart in his hands

He shows me he cares

Dreaming to love him

Like our hearts are intertwined

Where passion and lust meet

And he would be mine

Dreaming of how he wants me

While missing my touch

He'd see each day as an adventure

And I'd never be too much

When I show him my heart

He will know I have meaning

Until that day comes

I'll keep on dreaming.

If you think of me

If it's 3 am, and you're awake

Send me that message in your head

If you're crawling through your blankets

And you wish I was in your bed

If it's a Tuesday night and you can't sleep

Hope thoughts of me fill you up

They make you smile from our last conversation

And you text me to say you're enough

If you feel a little lonely

And the silence is more than you can stand

I hope you wish I was there with you

Just to hold your hand

If you ever find yourself daydreaming

And my voice is what you hear

I wish you'd just tell me

You want to have me near

If my smile fills a void

That you didn't know was there

Just say so in a few words

To let me know you care

If you're at a loss for words

Because you can't stand that you're alone

Just come snuggle up to me

I'll make you feel at home

If it's ever 3 am

And you stare at the ceiling

Just know that I'm there

And I know how you're feeling

Options

You're not my option

What if you're the one

What if I loved you and meant it

After all was said and done

If I treated you like my only

Why did you run away

If I asked to be your only one

Would you even stay

You're not my option

Because I chose you

I wanted to be your everything

I only wanted you

You were not my option

Because I saw your soul

From the moment I kissed you

Until you let me go

You were not my option

Because I put you first

I wouldve crawled through the desert

Just to quench your thirst

I became an option

When there was something else

Now you're my option

Because I already choose myself

Lyrics are a love language

Music

Run your smooth fingers over the jagged cracks of my soul

Find the flaws in my broken heart

Let me find the beauty in yours

Healing me from the inside out

With your words and poetry

The lyrics of your song

Plays with the beats of my heart

I hear you in my head, I see u in my dreams

You fill my thoughts like my favorite song

The drum of your voice is the beat

And you are the rhythm

You're the music to my soul

The chord that only I can hear

If this only exists in my dreams

Let me continue to sleep

I gotta be

I wanna be his everything

Give him the energy he emits

I wanna be the one that he needs

The kind that he can't be without

I wanna be the four am call

Just to say he needs me

The one he can't stop thinking about

When hes alone in his bed

I wanna be the kind of love

That he sees his forever in

The one that he knows

Will never leave

I wanna be the reason he wakes up

With a smile on his face

I wanna be the open heart

He tells his secrets to

I wanna be the arms he runs into

When the world has let him down

I wanna be the comfort he feels

When his life has gotten rough

I wanna be the best friend he has

And the one he laughs with

I´gotta be the one he wants

Because it's a must

And if he don't wanna be that for me

I'll hide my heart a while longer

Until I know I gotta be

The one he can't be without

Not yours

I'm not yours

You told me that

But if I'm not

Why do you kiss me like you do

You're not mine

I'm fine with that

But why does my mind

Constantly think of you

If you're not for me,

Why do you give me butterflies

If you don't want to be mine

Why do I dream of you

You're my first thought when I wake

The one I think of to sleep

Your voice offers me comfort

When silence is too loud

If you werent meant for me

How did our paths cross?

Why do you stay on my mind

And in my heart and soul.

If I'm not yours,

Why do I wanna be

Why don't I want anyone else

Inside my heart, my mind and my body

If you didn't intend to make me yours

I wish it would've never been

Because now I'm yours

And I'm scared that you'll never know

You won't know that you make me smile

Even when I don't want to

That you're a lyric to a song

That I haven't written

You're like a melody

That only I can hear

You're touch strums the instrument

That plays the tune in my heart

If you don't want to be mine

I'll live with that thought

But I want to be yours

And I'll wait for my moment

Home

Home isn't where you live

It's what's in your heart

The memories that flood you

Even when your family parts

The winding country roads

They always take me back

The smell of hay being cut

Our old go cart track

The pond where we went fishing

The scent of fresh mowed grass

Sunday supper at mamaws

Are all things of the past

Sometimes the memories fade

Until something reminds us

From the time we are born

Til the last day on the school bus

Memories are all that we have

As tears come from our eyes

They serve as constant reminders

Of our hardest goodbyes.

They sometimes bring back laughter

Without them smiles can't be found

When you get where you're going

Don't forget to turn back around.

His reflection

He is just like a book

With pages that tell his life

He's fit to be a king

Deserves to make someone his wife

His touch is so soft and caring

He's deeper than he shows

He cares about people around him

His heart could overflow

He's scared of meeting someone

That doesn't get his fantasies

The ones he holds back

Where could she be

He's dreaming of that someone

That don't mind who he is

Someone to build a life with

And wants to have his kids

He don't want to share her with anyone

This man that's worth her time

At night he sleeps with the question

When can I make her mine?

She'd love to hold him all night

Just to hear him breathe

She's always wanted someone

That never wanted to leave

What she wouldn't give

For those catch your breath moments

The ones that make you miss him

The ones with the best intent

She waits for him to make a move

Because she is too scared to confess

But her memories of him

Are what serves her best

Lonely

Silence is the loudest

When you realize you're alone

No chest to lay your head on

No heart to call home

Boredom is the worse

When it's three in the morning

Noone around to talk to

Life can be so boring

Chaos is the most stressful

When you don't have a friend

You search for the solution

But can't find the end

Enduring takes talent

To put on a brave face

Knowing that you will fall apart

When you find your safe space

Loving takes generosity

When you give more than you get

When you beg for more attention

Realizing it's not your turn yet

Pain is a heart broken

Not knowing what to do

And that's the worse emotion

When it comes to me and you.

Body Language

I can read your body language

From across the room

You think youre my game

You don't trust me, do you?

You don't show me the affection

That you once did

The things you had made me feel

Now you keep them hid

I question what I did to you

To make you turn it off

We'd been vibin so well

Now you have just stopped

No more kissing or holding me

I guess there's someone else

The heart I once felt beat

I haven't really felt

This was my fear of love

Coming through in waves

It's how I always know

I'm getting played.

You think I'm just playing you

But I'm giving you my best

I've faded all the other guys

Don't want the rest

I could've been what you needed

But rejection has became clear

I just want to text you and say

I always wish you were here

www.ingramcontent.com/pod-product-compliance
Lightning Source LLC
LaVergne TN
LVHW100328181026
850499LV00039B/1018
9789354589126